COMIC STRIP FUN

ACKNOWLEDGEMENT

The authors, Carolyn Davis and Charlene Brown, would like to thank all of the following for their patience and support: Sally Black, Sally Marshall Corngold, Pat Brown and our friends at Marian Bergeson Elementary and of course, the wonderful staff at Walter Foster Publishing.

INTRODUCTION

Comics strips are a fun way to tell a story or joke. By using different characters, facial expressions and body movements, you can tell a complete story in just a few frames. You can even tell a quick joke in a single frame. The old saying "a picture is worth a thousand words" is certainly true!

This book makes drawing comics easy! All the examples of heads, bodies, arms and legs are interchangeable. You can use an unlimited variety of combinations to create any mood you want for your character. And, since all the parts are interchangeable, you need only to trace or copy your characters. How easy and fun!

While you are having fun making comic strips, you are also learning how to draw and how to write a story. You can use comic strips not only to tell humorous stories, but also to tell serious stories. You may find this a good way to express your feelings about something in your life, or you may find it a fun way to do school projects.

Remember, the characters and expressions in this book are just some ideas you can use. So, use your imagination to make up your own characters and situations. And please, HAVE FUN!

GLOSSARY

Body Movements—Actions that show emotion or feeling. A character waving his arms would, perhaps, show a feeling of excitement.

Character—A person or animal in your cartoon. Each character has a distinct or different personality.

Comic—Humorous art. The Sunday comics are actually art pieces or illustrations.

Details—A small part of the whole character which adds personality, such as eyes, nose, mouth and clothes. By adding a large red nose, a pointed hat and a costume with large buttons to a character, the readers knows the character is a clown.

Expressions—A showing of feeling or emotion. In comic strips you will use both facial and body expressions.

Facial Movements—Facial actions that shows emotion. The character's emotion was seen in his facial movements as his expression went from surprise to pleasure.

Frame—One section of a comic strip. Each frame or box tells a part of the whole story.

Prop—An object that helps establish the character's personality or the overall situation. The clown's props would be juggling balls or balloons.

Rough Sketch—Light pencil drawing of the comic. We suggest that you first draw a rough sketch in light pencil, then go over the pencil in ink, then erase the pencil. This saves you from having to redo the drawing because of a mistake.

Setting—The background surrounding that sets time, area or situation. For example, to show your reader that the time is prehistoric, you might draw a dinosaur in the background. You may want to draw a doghouse as setting for your dog character.

CONTENTS

MATERIALS

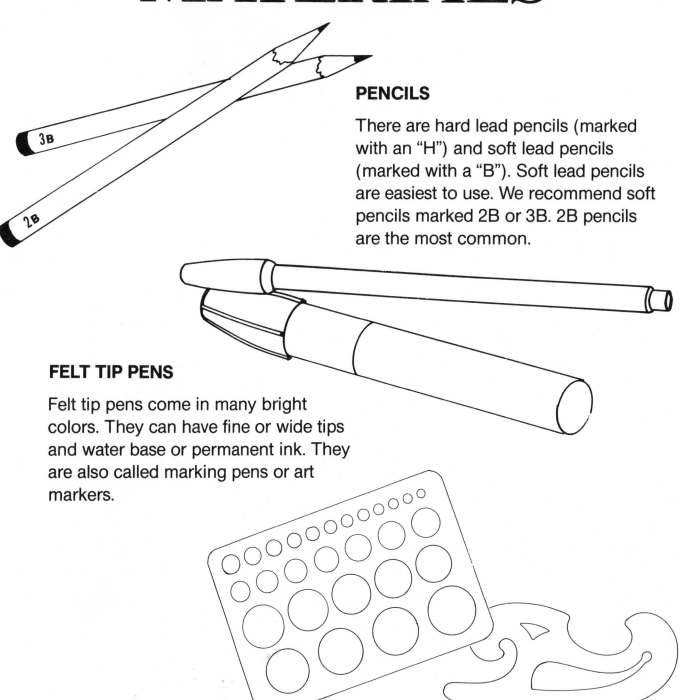

PENCILS

There are hard lead pencils (marked with an "H") and soft lead pencils (marked with a "B"). Soft lead pencils are easiest to use. We recommend soft pencils marked 2B or 3B. 2B pencils are the most common.

FELT TIP PENS

Felt tip pens come in many bright colors. They can have fine or wide tips and water base or permanent ink. They are also called marking pens or art markers.

TEMPLATES

Templates are used for making perfect ovals, circles, curves and other shapes. They come in many different designs.

MATERIALS

PAPER

Any drawing paper can be used for drawing comics. Drawing paper comes in pads or packages of single sheets.

TRACING PAPER

Tracing paper comes in different sizes and different weights. Heavy weight is best.

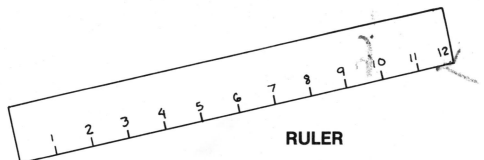

RULER

The ruler is used for measuring and drawing straight lines.

1.

FACIAL EXPRESSIONS

One of the most important ways to tell how your characters feel or what your characters are doing is by the expressions on their faces. In this chapter we are going to learn how different faces can express happiness, sadness, anger, amazement, fright, or anything you want. We will show you how to draw all kinds of fun expressions to help you tell your story or joke. You can copy or trace the expressions and faces we show you, or use your imagination to make up your own.

HEADS

Your character's head can be egg shaped, round or rectangular. It can be short and wide or long and thin. Think about how you want your character's head to look. Draw the head.

EXAMPLES YOU MIGHT USE:

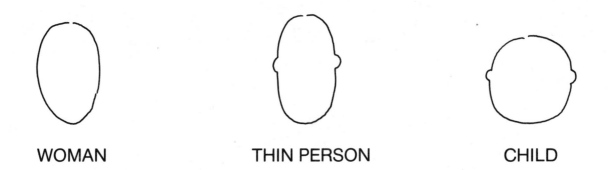

WOMAN   THIN PERSON   CHILD

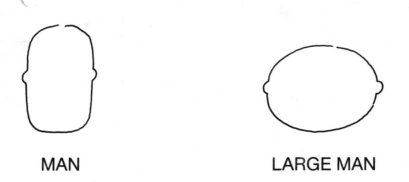

MAN   LARGE MAN

10.

DETAILS

Details can tell a lot about your character's emotions and thoughts. Decide what kind of expression you want your character to have. Draw the eyes, nose and mouth.

NOSES:

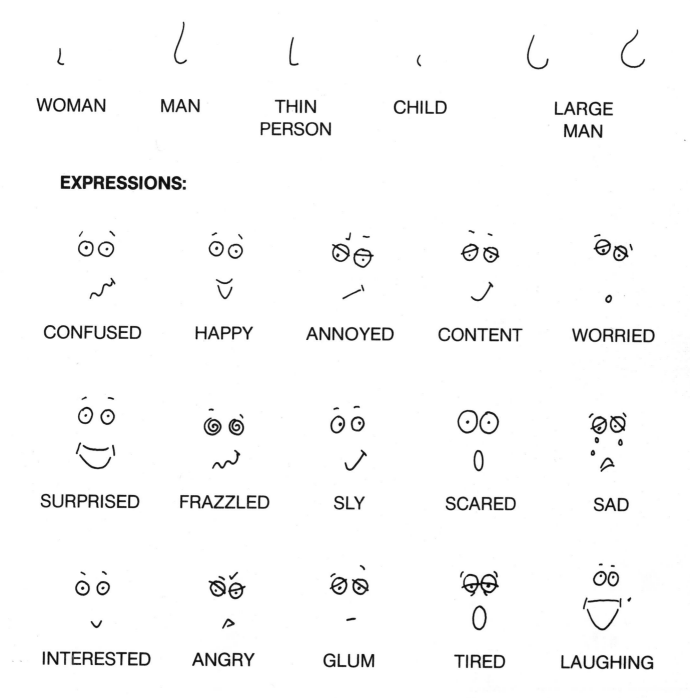

WOMAN MAN THIN PERSON CHILD LARGE MAN

EXPRESSIONS:

CONFUSED HAPPY ANNOYED CONTENT WORRIED

SURPRISED FRAZZLED SLY SCARED SAD

INTERESTED ANGRY GLUM TIRED LAUGHING

FACES

Here are examples of facial expressions for different types of characters. You can copy or trace these, or make up your own.

UNHAPPY
LARGE
MAN

SILLY
LARGE
MAN

PLEASED
LARGE
MAN

PASSIVE
LARGE
MAN

LAUGHING
MAN

FRAZZLED
MAN

ANGRY
MAN

SAD
CHILD

HAPPY
CHILD

TIRED
CHILD

LAUGHING
CHILD

**CONFUSED
MAN**

**SURPRISED
MAN**

**ANNOYED
MAN**

**CONTENT
MAN**

**TIRED
MAN**

**BEFUDDLED
MAN**

**AMAZED
MAN**

**SCARED
WOMAN**

**SAD
WOMAN**

**NICE
WOMAN**

**ANGRY
WOMAN**

**LAZY
WOMAN**

13.

HAIR

You can make your character's hair long, short, curly or straight. It can be blowing in the wind, styled in pigtails, or standing on end. Here are some examples:

MEN

LARGE
MEN

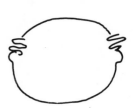

14.

THIN MEN

WOMEN

GIRLS

BOYS

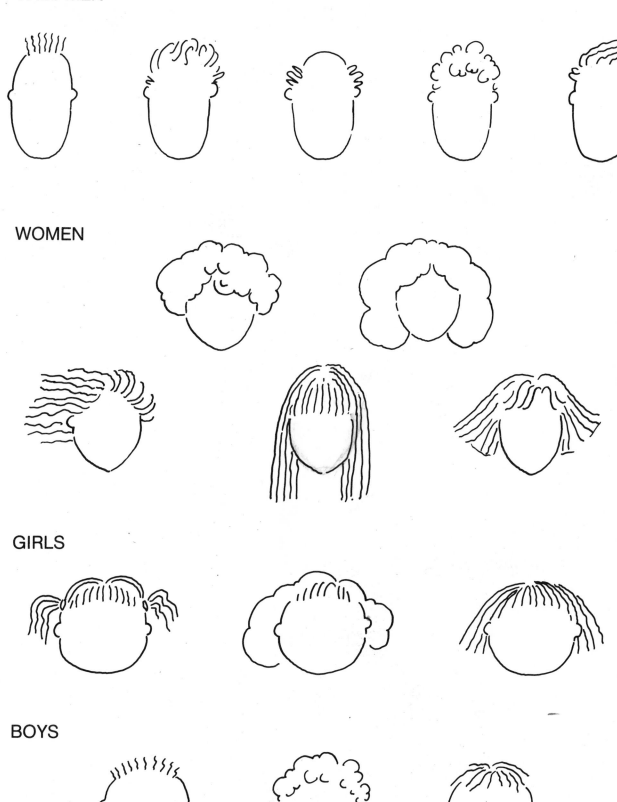

15.

16.

2.

BODY MOVEMENTS

Now that we know how to make faces and facial expressions, we need to learn how to draw bodies and body movements. In this chapter, we will learn how to put a head and face together with a body, and even clothes, to further express our character's thoughts and emotions. For instance, we can draw a body leaping into the air with waving arms for a happy, excited man, or we can give a frowning woman a body with her hands on her hips to show anger or impatience.

You may trace or copy the examples in this book, or use your imagination to create other body expressions that will help tell your stories and jokes.

PEOPLE

After you have decided what type of emotion or thought you want your character to express, draw a body that will go with the character's facial expression. You can trace or copy our examples, putting the details together with the body.

MEN: Men's bodies are rectangular with large shoulders, hands and feet.

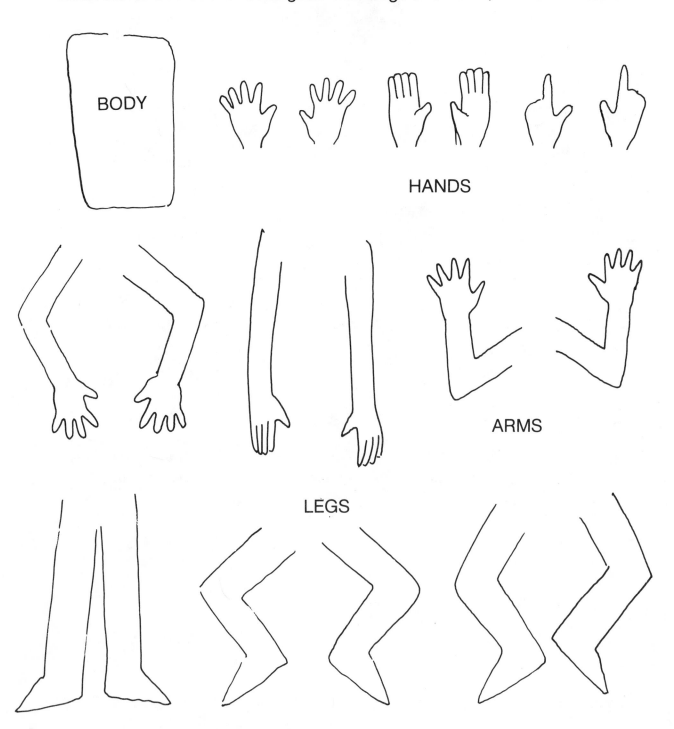

BODY

HANDS

ARMS

LEGS

Notice how the various positions of the hands, arms and legs create different emotions. Try using different facial expressions with the same body to see how you can change the meaning of the body's movements.

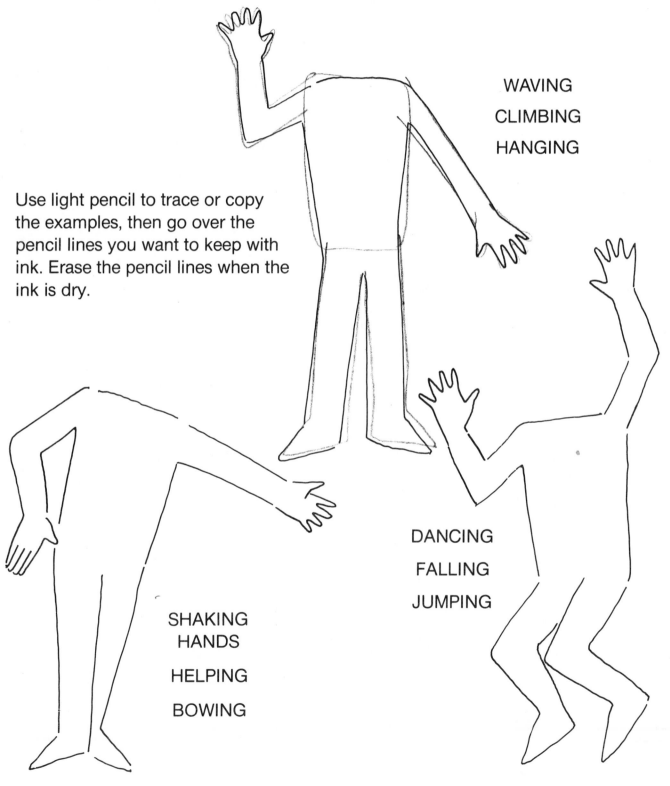

WAVING

CLIMBING

HANGING

Use light pencil to trace or copy the examples, then go over the pencil lines you want to keep with ink. Erase the pencil lines when the ink is dry.

DANCING

FALLING

JUMPING

SHAKING
HANDS

HELPING

BOWING

19.

THIN OR TALL PEOPLE: Thin, tall people have long, thin arms, legs and hands.

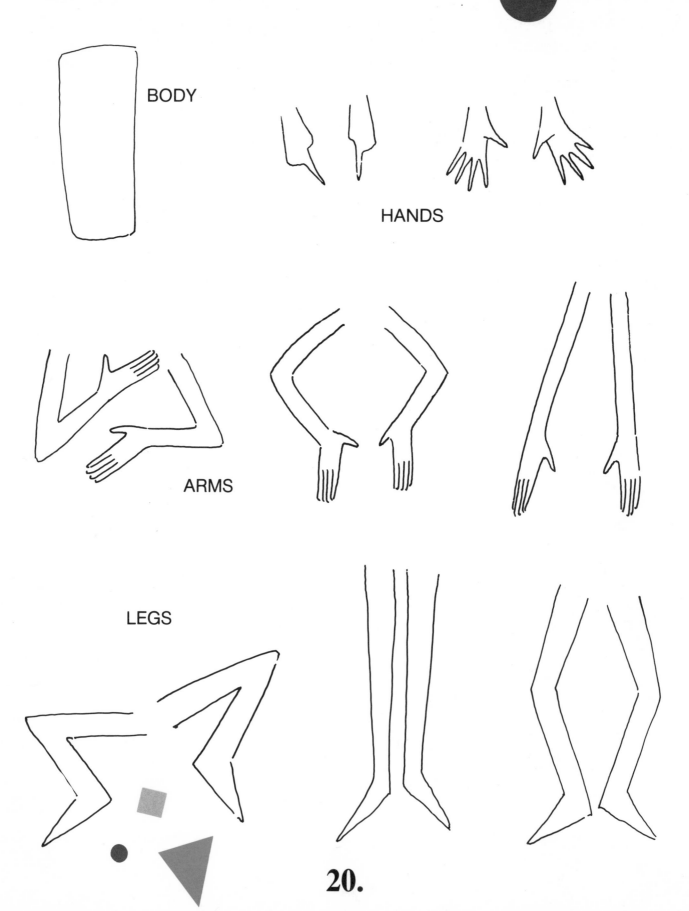

BODY

HANDS

ARMS

LEGS

20.

These body movements show different emotions when used with different facial expressions. Try drawing different faces on each of these examples.

Use light pencil to trace or copy the examples, then go over the pencil lines you want to keep with ink. Erase the pencil lines when the ink is dry.

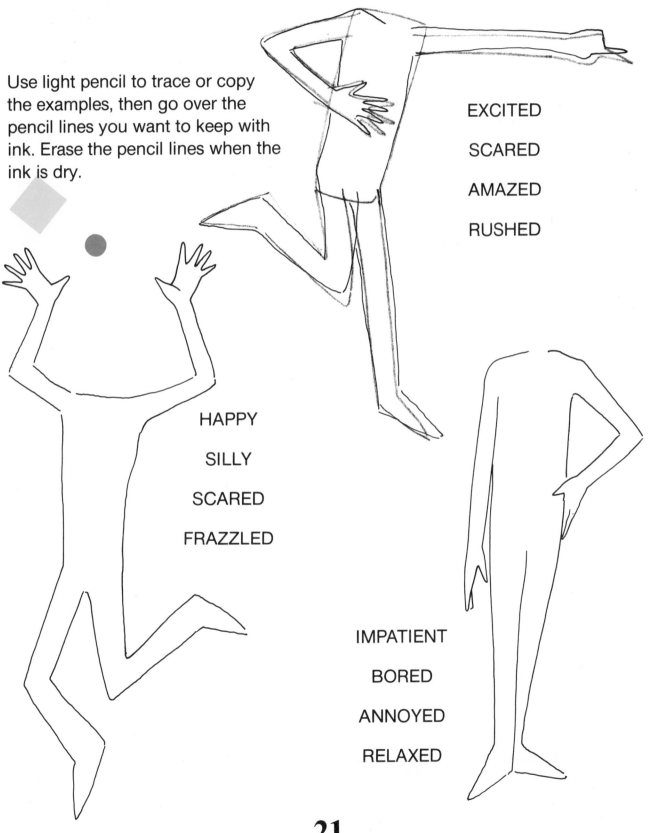

EXCITED

SCARED

AMAZED

RUSHED

HAPPY

SILLY

SCARED

FRAZZLED

IMPATIENT

BORED

ANNOYED

RELAXED

CHILDREN: Children have smaller, shorter and rounder features than adults.

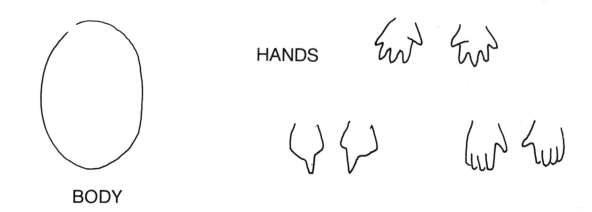

BODY

HANDS

ARMS

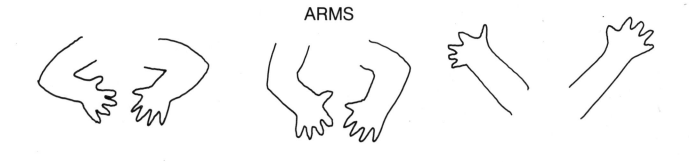

LEGS

Use light pencil to trace or copy the examples, then go over the pencil lines you want to keep with ink. Erase the pencil lines when the ink is dry.

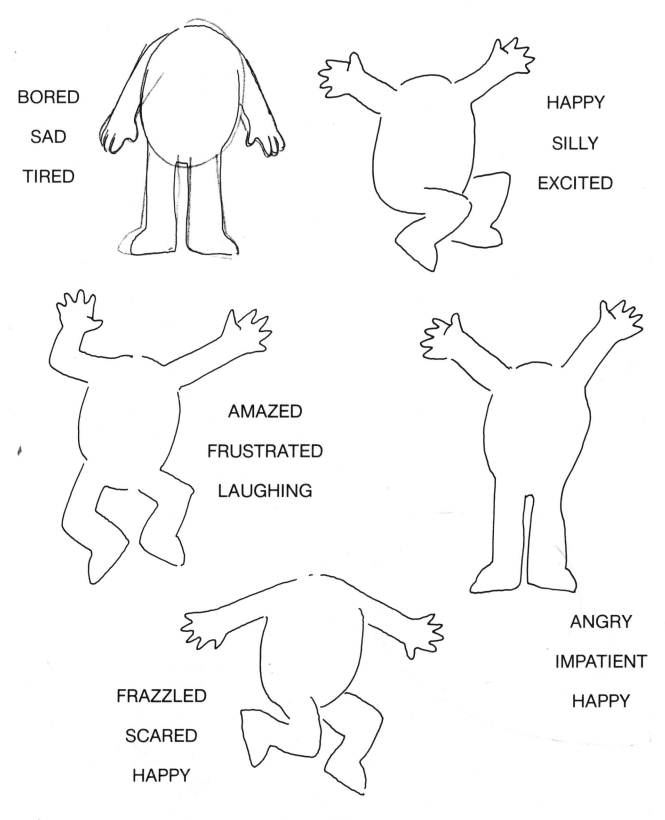

BORED

SAD

TIRED

HAPPY

SILLY

EXCITED

AMAZED

FRUSTRATED

LAUGHING

ANGRY

IMPATIENT

HAPPY

FRAZZLED

SCARED

HAPPY

23.

WOMEN: Women have thin waists, wide hips and narrow shoulders. Their hands, arms and legs are small and slender.

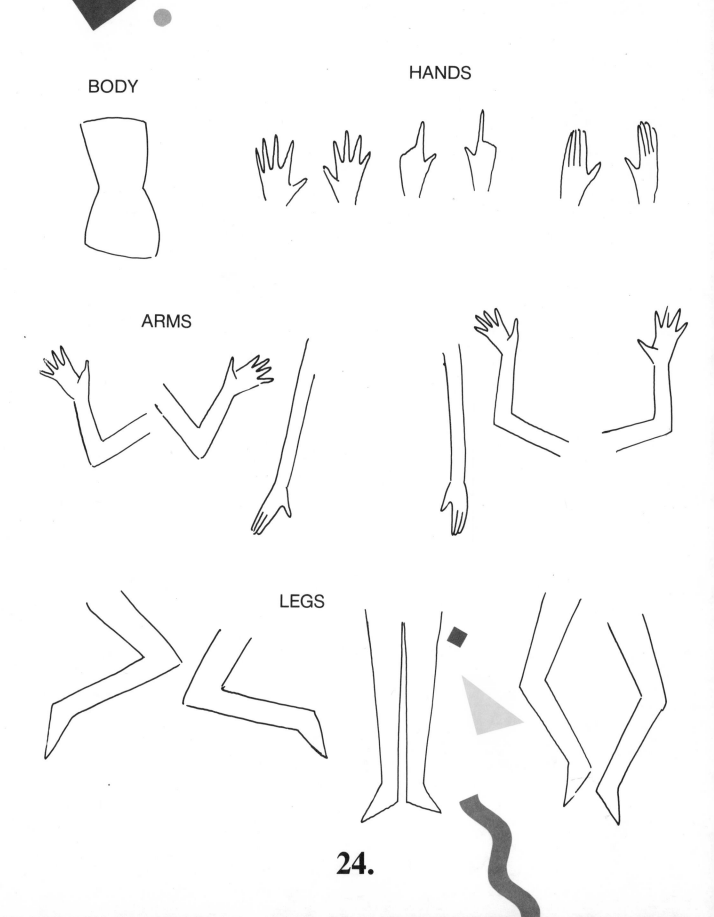

BODY

HANDS

ARMS

LEGS

24.

Use light pencil to trace or copy the examples, then go over the pencil lines you want to keep with ink. Erase the pencil lines when the ink is dry.

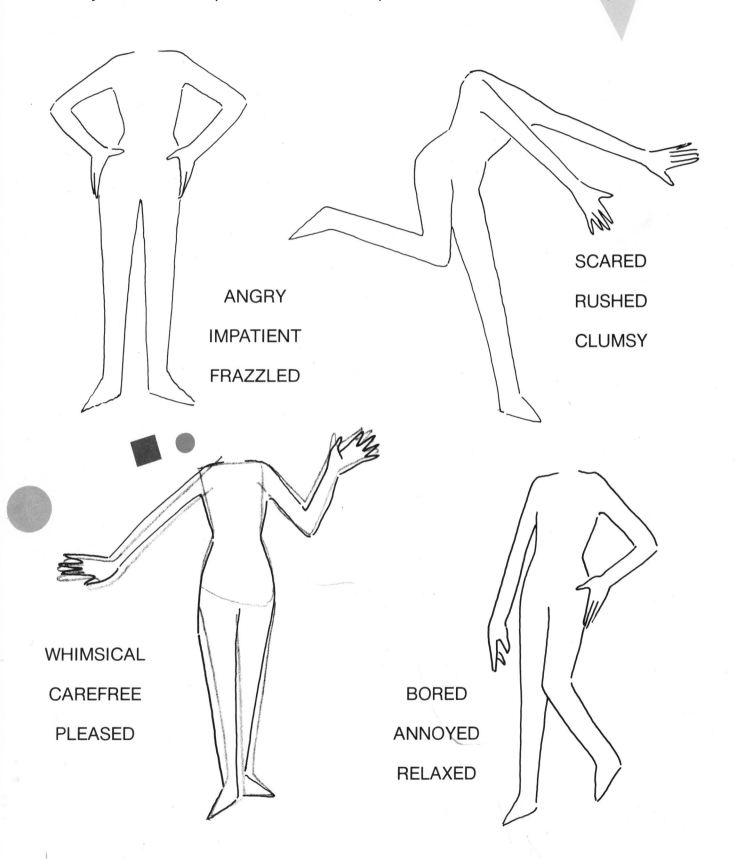

ANGRY

IMPATIENT

FRAZZLED

SCARED

RUSHED

CLUMSY

WHIMSICAL

CAREFREE

PLEASED

BORED

ANNOYED

RELAXED

25.

See how the characters look with all the shapes put together. Notice how the bodies of the men, women and children are all different. Copy or trace these examples, then try drawing some characters on your own.

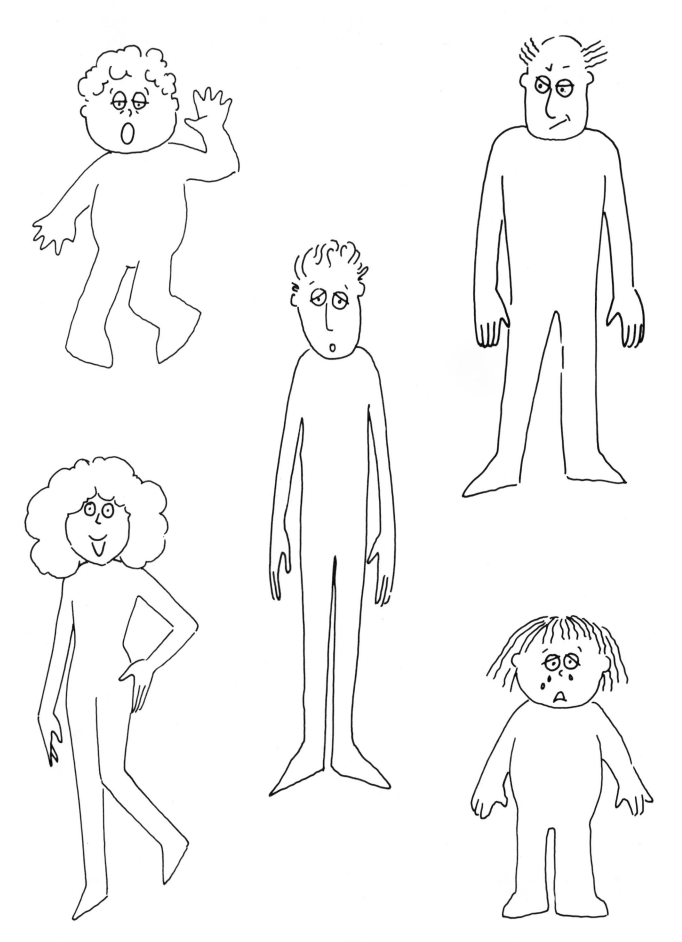

27.

ANIMALS

Animals are fun to draw and can show expression just like people.

BODY PARTS

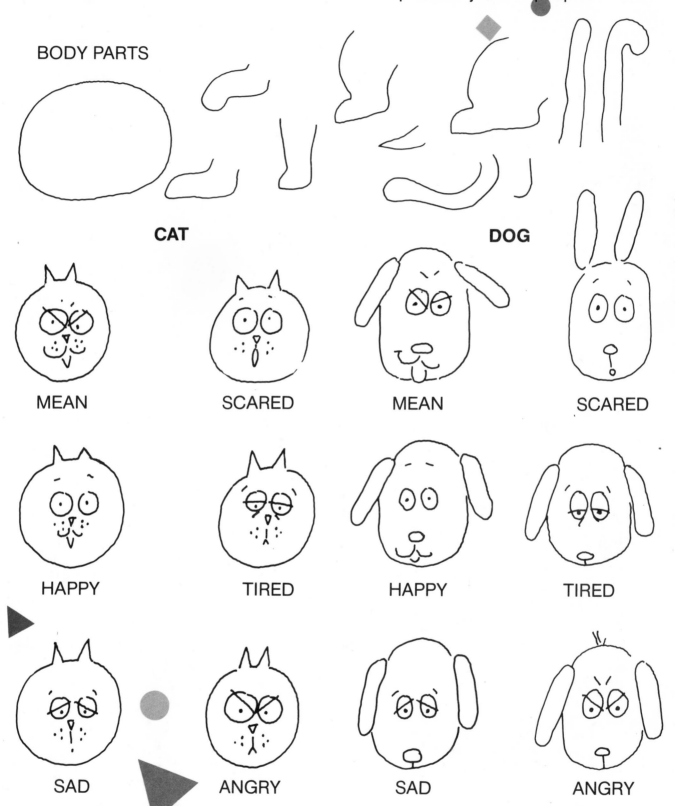

CAT   **DOG**

MEAN   SCARED   MEAN   SCARED

HAPPY   TIRED   HAPPY   TIRED

SAD   ANGRY   SAD   ANGRY

28.

Try putting the body parts together with the faces.

Use light pencil to trace or copy the examples, then go over the pencil lines you want to keep with ink. Erase the pencil lines when the ink is dry.

CATS

Here are some facial and body expressions for a cat. Copy or trace these examples or use your imagination to make up your own.

SLEEPY

ANGRY

SCARED

PLAYFUL

MEAN

30.

DOGS

Here are some facial and body expressions for a dog. Copy or trace these examples or use your imagination to make up your own.

SAD

BORED

CRAZY

HAPPY

31.

Clothes can add a lot of personality to your characters. They can often explain why your character is acting a certain way, or why your character is in a particular situation. Clothing can show what your character's occupation is, how old your character is, and, sometimes, even what your character is thinking.

Lightly sketch your character with light pencil, then sketch the clothing over the character with pencil, then ink over the lines you want to keep. Erase any pencil lines. Now you can color your character if you wish.

We've added clothes and sunglasses to this character, creating "Mr. Cool," running off to join his friends for some fun after school.

CHARACTER

Here, tights and a blue cape have made our character into a super hero on his way to fight crime.

This poor cat doesn't look very happy in his t-shirt and cap. Maybe he's all dressed up with no place to go!?

Lightly sketch your character with light pencil, then sketch the clothing over the character with pencil, adding details to create more expression. Ink over the lines you want to keep, then erase any pencil lines. Now you can color your character if you wish.

A fun costume changes this happy man into a jolly clown.

Adding a fancy dress and
a crown to this character
creates a fairy princess.

This little boy needs a shirt,
shorts and shoes before he
can go outside to play.

35.

36.

3.

CHARACTER INTERACTION

In this chapter, we will learn how two or more characters interact with each other. By putting the characters together, we can tell or show different stories and jokes. This works by using the facial expressions and body movements that we learned in previous chapters. We will also learn how to make simple line drawings of furniture, rooms and scenery to better explain our stories.

This is where drawing comics is really fun! Remember, you must think out your story and characters before you begin to draw. Also, this is a bit more difficult, so to make it easier, start with pencil.

PUTTING CHARACTERS

Putting two or more characters together can make a story by itself. Here are some examples. Use your imagination to make up different stories they might be telling.

TOGETHER

SUPER HERO

PROPS AND SCENERY

Here are some props and scenery you might want to use. Notice that they are drawn with simple lines to give just an idea of the setting.

VASE

DOOR

DOG HOUSE

WINDOW

CHAIR

40.

CLOUD

TREE

WASTE BASKET

CHAIR

CITYSCAPE

41.

DRAW YOUR CHARACTER WITH PROPS

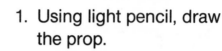

1. Using light pencil, draw the prop.
2. Using light pencil, draw your character over the prop.

3. Draw over the lines you want to keep with ink.

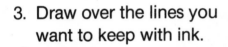

4. Erase the pencil lines.

1. Using light pencil, draw the prop.
2. Using light pencil, draw your character over the prop.

3. Draw over the lines you want to keep with ink.
4. Erase the pencil lines.

43.

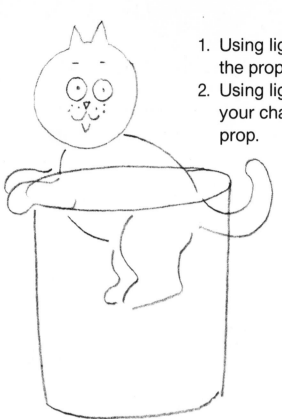

1. Using light pencil, draw the prop.
2. Using light pencil, draw your character over the prop.

3. Draw over the lines you want to keep with ink.
4. Erase the pencil lines.

5. Color your drawing. You may use felt tip pens, crayons, colored pencils or watercolor paints.

1. Using light pencil, draw the prop.
2. Using light pencil, draw your character over the prop.

3. Draw over the lines you want to keep with ink.
4. Erase the pencil lines.

5. Color your drawing. You may use felt tip pens, crayons, colored pencils or watercolor paints.

45.

BACKGROUNDS, PROPS

1. Draw your picture in pencil. Overlap the background and props if you need to.
2. Draw over the lines you want to keep with ink. Erase the pencil lines.

46.

AND CHARACTERS

1. Draw your picture in pencil. Overlap the background and props if you need to.
2. Draw over the lines you want to keep with ink. Erase the pencil lines.

47.

4.

MAKE A STORY

Now we are going to use everything we learned in the previous chapters to make a complete comic strip. You can trace your characters in each frame of the strip, or use your imagination to draw them on your own.

The most important part of drawing comics is to think out your story, then break it into separate parts or frames. You must illustrate your characters carefully, using the proper expressions and body movements to make sure the meaning of your joke or story comes out the way you want it to.

PUTTING A STORY

1. Decide what story or joke you want to tell.
2. Write down your story or joke.
3. Break your story into parts, each part will be a separate frame.
4. Decide what characters, expressions and body movements will best illustrate each part of your story. Draw or trace some rough sketches for each frame.

Example:
Frame 1 — Cat watching dog fly. Dog not watching where he's going.
Frame 2 — Man waves arms, tries to warn dog.
Frame 3 — Dog flies into building and slides down.

CHARACTERS FOR FRAME 1

TOGETHER

CHARACTER FOR FRAME 2

CHARACTER FOR FRAME 3

5. After you have decided which rough drawing works best for each part, you can draw the frames for your comic strip. The size we have used here best fits our earlier drawings. Then, you can start drawing your characters.

EXAMPLE: FRAME 1

6. Carefully draw your characters in pencil. Be sure to leave enough space for words if you need to.

EXAMPLE: FRAME 1

7. Using pencil, draw the props and the bubbles for the words.
8. When your pencil drawing is complete, ink over the lines you want to keep, then erase the pencil lines.

EXAMPLE: FRAME 1

9. Now you can color your comic strip if you wish. If you used tracing paper for your drawing, you might want to use colored pencils, crayons or felt tip pens. If you used drawing paper, you can also use watercolor paints.

EXAMPLE: FRAME 1

FINISHED

Notice how the characters' facial expressions and body movements tell the story with very few words.

COMIC STRIP

MAKE ANOTHER

1. Think out your story and write it down.
2. Break your story into parts. Each part will become a separate frame.

   1. Mom yelling at boy for playing music too loud.
   2. Boy is puzzled because he's not playing music.
   3. Dog is in other room rockin' out to music.

STORY

3. Draw the characters and props in each frame with pencil, then ink over the lines you want to keep. Erase the pencil lines when the ink is dry.
4. Write in words if necessary.

SINGLE FRAME

Sometimes you can tell your story or joke in just one frame. This is called a single frame comic. Facial expressions, body movements and props are very important in single frame comics.

CAT - A - LOG

CAT - E - CORNERED

COMICS

CAT - A - LIST

CAT - TAS - TROPHE

Here are some more examples of single frame comics. See if you can think of some "Historical Footnotes" on your own.